SandCastle 3

Homographs

Fruit Trees Produce Produce

Carey Molter

ABDO
Publishing Company

Published by SandCastle™, an imprint of ABDO Publishing Company, 4940 Viking Drive, Edina, Minnesota 55435.

Cover and interior photo credits: Comstock, Digital Vision, Eyewire Images, John Foxx Images, PhotoDisc, Rubberball Productions, Stockbyte

Library of Congress Cataloging-in-Publication Data

Molter, Carey, 1973-
    Fruit trees produce produce / Carey Molter.
        p. cm. -- (Homographs)
    Includes index.
    Summary: Photographs and simple text introduce homophones, words with different meanings that are spelled the same but sound different.
    ISBN 1-57765-794-2
    1. English language--Homonyms--Juvenile literature. [1. English language--Homonyms.]
I. Title.

PE1595 .M66 2002
428.1--dc21

                                                                    2001053318

The SandCastle concept, content, and reading method have been reviewed and approved by a national advisory board including literacy specialists, librarians, elementary school teachers, early childhood education professionals, and parents.

Let Us Know

After reading the book, SandCastle would like you to tell us your stories about reading. What is your favorite page? Was there something hard that you needed help with? Share the ups and downs of learning to read. We want to hear from you! To get posted on the ABDO Publishing Company Web site, send us email at:

sandcastle@abdopub.com

About SandCastle™

Nonfiction books for the beginning reader

- Basic concepts of phonics are incorporated with integrated language methods of reading instruction. Most words are short, and phrases, letter sounds, and word sounds are repeated.

- Book levels are based on the ATOS™ for Books formula. Other considerations for readability include the number of words in each sentence, the number of characters in each word, and word lists based on curriculum frameworks.

- Full-color photography reinforces word meanings and concepts.

- "Words I Can Read" list at the end of each book teaches basic elements of grammar, helps the reader recognize the words in the text, and builds vocabulary.

- Reading levels are indicated by the number of flags on the castle.

SandCastle uses the following definitions for this series:

- Homographs: words that are spelled the same but sound different and have different meanings. *Easy memory tip: "-graph"= same look*

- Homonyms: words that are spelled and sound the same but have different meanings. *Easy memory tip: "-nym"= same name*

- Homophones: words that sound alike but are spelled differently and have different meanings. *Easy memory tip: "-phone"= sound alike*

Look for more SandCastle books in these three reading levels:

| **Level 1**
(one flag) | **Level 2**
(two flags) | **Level 3**
(three flags) |

| **Grades Pre-K to K**
5 or fewer words per page | **Grades K to 1**
5 to 10 words per page | **Grades 1 to 2**
10 to 15 words per page |

Note: Many of the pages in this book have fewer than 10 words due to the difficulty of the subject matter.

Homographs are words that are spelled the same but sound different and have different meanings.

We buy our fresh produce at a fruit stand.

He can produce a rabbit from his hat.

Kris and Jen **use** towels to cover up.

The bubble wand is in use.

Dad waits his turn.

Jim is close to the fence.

I close my eyes to keep the water out.

Does are female deer.

These two rest on the grass.

Mom does her best to hold on tight.

My grandma enjoys putting at the golf course.

Hank likes putting on face paint.

Luna will often subject her brother to tickle fights.

The subject of this book is cowboys.

Abel plays a video game.

The object of the game is to save the princess.

I do not **object** to sharing popcorn on movie night.

We will house the Clarks while they visit our city.

What is for sale?

(house)

Words I Can Read

Nouns

A noun is a person, place, or thing

best (BEST) p. 13
book (BUK) p. 17
brother (BRUHTH-ur) p. 16
bubble (BUH-buhl) p. 9
city (SIT-ee) p. 20
cowboys (KOU-boiz) p. 17
deer (DIHR) p. 12
does (DOHZ) p. 12
eyes (EYEZ) p. 11
face (FAYSS) p. 15
fence (FENSS) p. 10
fights (FITESS) p. 16
fruit (FROOT) p. 6
game (GAYM) p. 18
golf course (GOLF KORSS) p. 14

grandma (GRAND-mah) p. 14
grass (GRASS) p. 12
hat (HAT) p. 7
homographs (HOM-uh-grafss) p. 5
house (HOUSS) p. 21
meanings (MEE-ningz) p. 5
movie (MOO-vee) p. 19
night (NITE) p. 19
object (OB-jikt) p. 18
paint (PAYNT) p. 15
popcorn (POP-korn) p. 19
princess (PRIN-sess) p. 18

produce (PROH-dooss) p. 6
rabbit (RAB-it) p. 7
sale (SAYL) p. 21
stand (STAND) p. 6
subject (SUHB-jikt) p. 17
towels (TOU-uhlz) p. 8
turn (TURN) p. 9
use (YOOSS) p. 9
video game (VID-ee-oh GAYM) p. 18
wand (WOND) p. 9
water (WAW-tur) p. 11
words (WURDZ) p. 5

Proper Nouns

A proper noun is the name of a person, place, or thing

Abel (AY-buhl) p. 18
Clarks (KLARKSS) p. 20
Dad (DAD) p. 9

Hank (HANGK) p. 15
Jen (JEN) p. 8
Jim (JIM) p. 10

Kris (KRISS) p. 8
Luna (LOO-nuh) p. 16
Mom (MOM) p. 13

Pronouns
A pronoun is a word that replaces a noun

he (HEE) p. 7
I (EYE) pp. 11, 19

they (THAY) p. 20
two (TOO) p. 12

we (WEE) pp. 6, 20
what (WUHT) p. 21

Verbs
A verb is an action or being word

are (AR) pp. 5, 12
buy (BYE) p. 6
can (KAN) p. 7
close (KLOHZ) p. 11
cover (KUHV-ur) p. 8
do (DOO) p. 19
does (DUHZ) p. 13
enjoys (en-JOIZ) p. 14
have (HAV) p. 5
hold on (HOHLD ON)
   p. 13
house (HOUZ) p. 20

is (IZ)
   pp. 9, 10, 17, 18, 21
keep (KEEP) p. 11
likes (LIKESS) p. 15
object (uhb-JEKT) p. 19
plays (PLAYZ) p. 18
produce
   (pruh-DOOSS) p. 7
putting (PUHT-ing)
   p. 14
putting (PUT-ing) p. 15
rest (REST) p. 12

save (SAYV) p. 18
sharing (SHAIR-ing)
   p. 19
sound (SOUND) p. 5
spelled (SPELD) p. 5
subject (suhb-JEKT)
   p. 16
tickle (TIK-uhl) p. 16
use (YOOZ) p. 8
visit (VIZ-it) p. 20
waits (WAYTSS) p. 9
will (WIL) pp. 16, 20

Adjectives
An adjective describes something

different (DIF-ur-uhnt)
   p. 5
female (FEE-male)
   p. 12
fresh (FRESH) p. 6

her (HUR) pp. 13, 16
his (HIZ) pp. 7, 9
my (MYE) pp. 11, 14
our (OUR) pp. 6, 20
these (THEEZ) p. 12

this (THISS) p. 17
tight (TITE) p. 13

23

Adverbs

An adverb tells how, when, or where something happens

close (KLOHSS) p. 10   **on** (ON) p. 15   **same** (SAYM) p. 5
often (OF-uhn) p. 16   **out** (OUT) p. 11   **up** (UHP) p. 8